Doors of

Morocco

أبواب المغرب

Coffee Table
Photobook

Mosaic Tree Press

Published by
Mosaic Tree Press

In the name of God, the Most Gracious, the Most Merciful

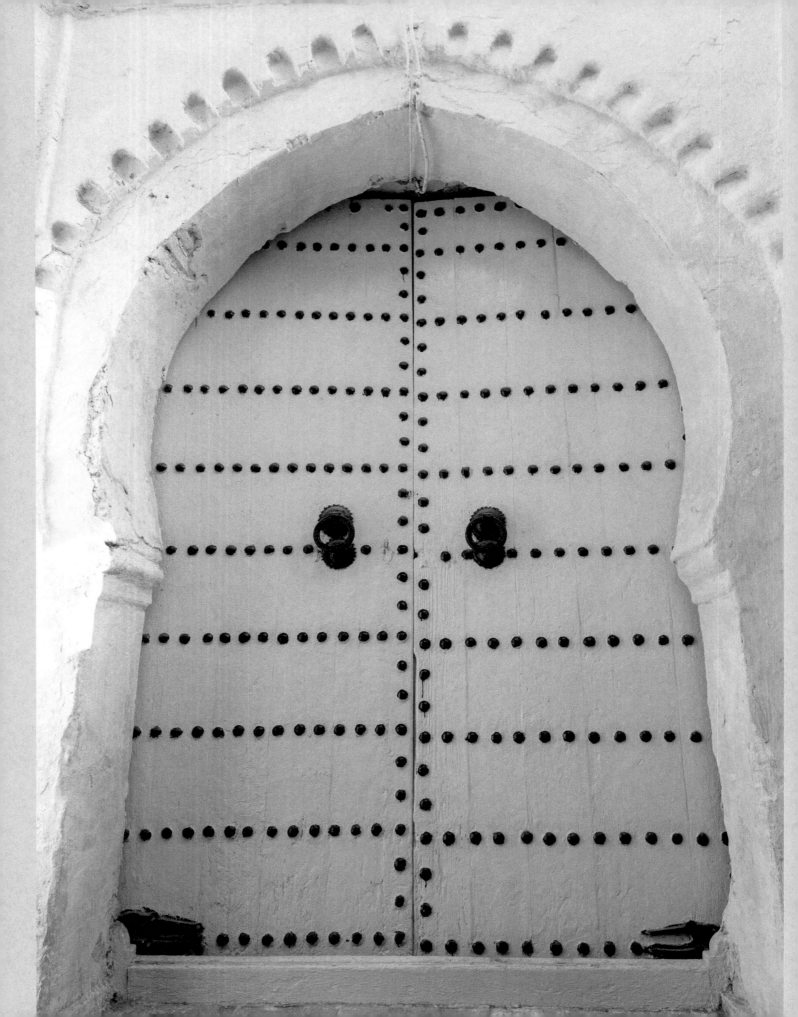

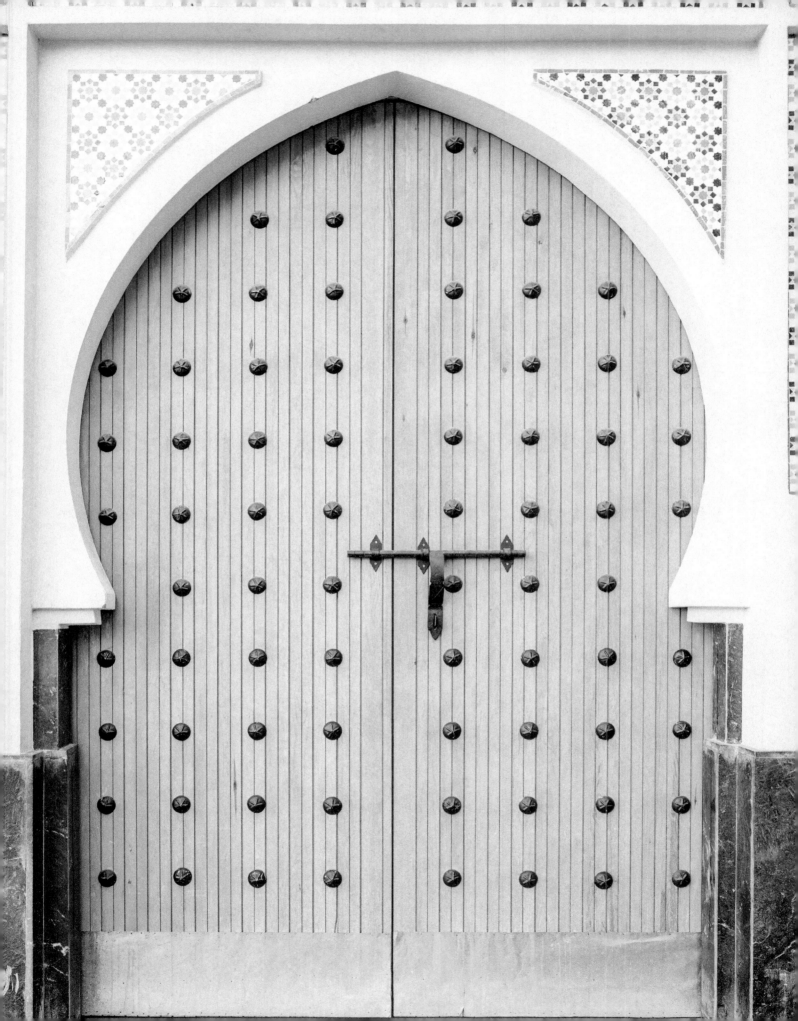

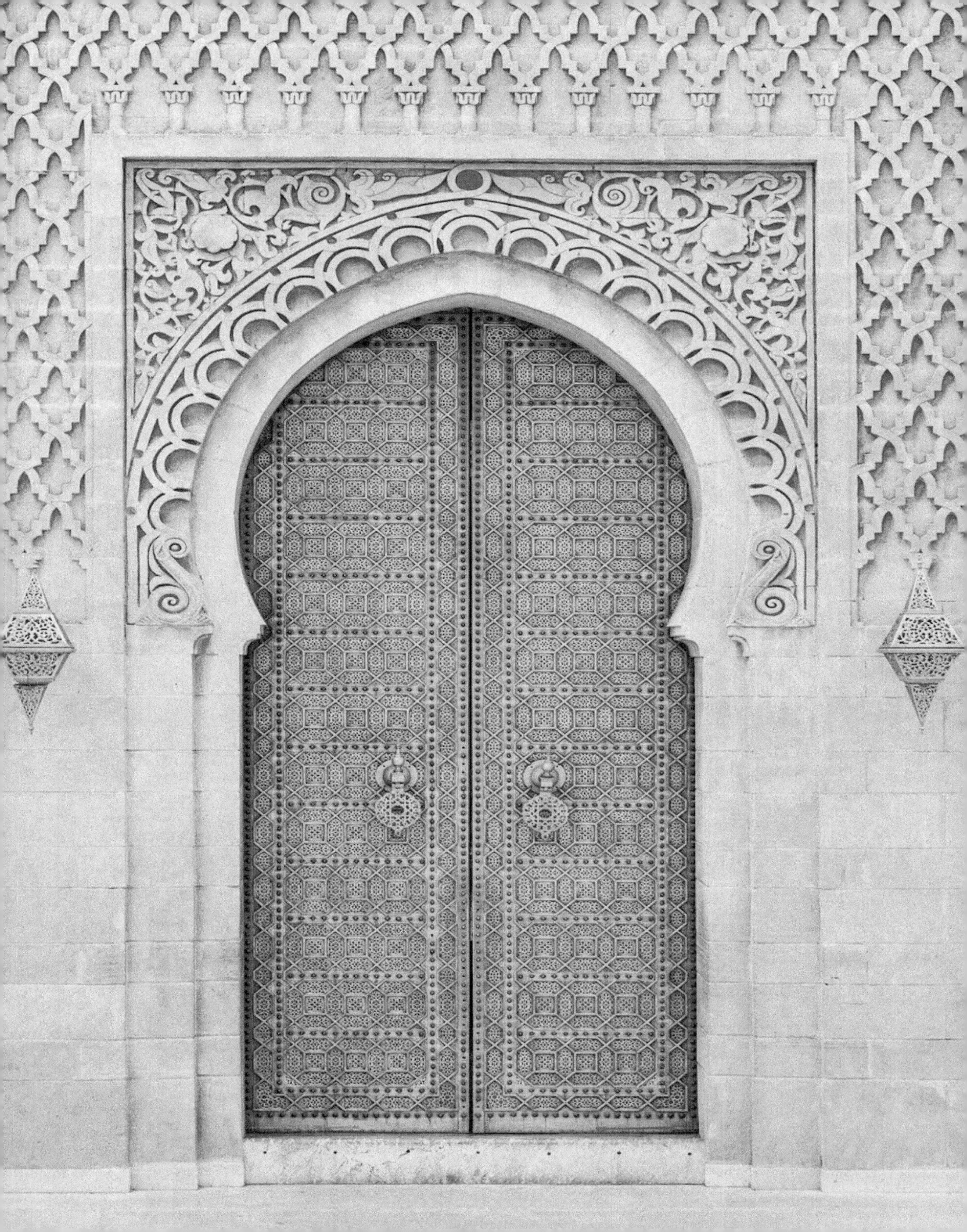

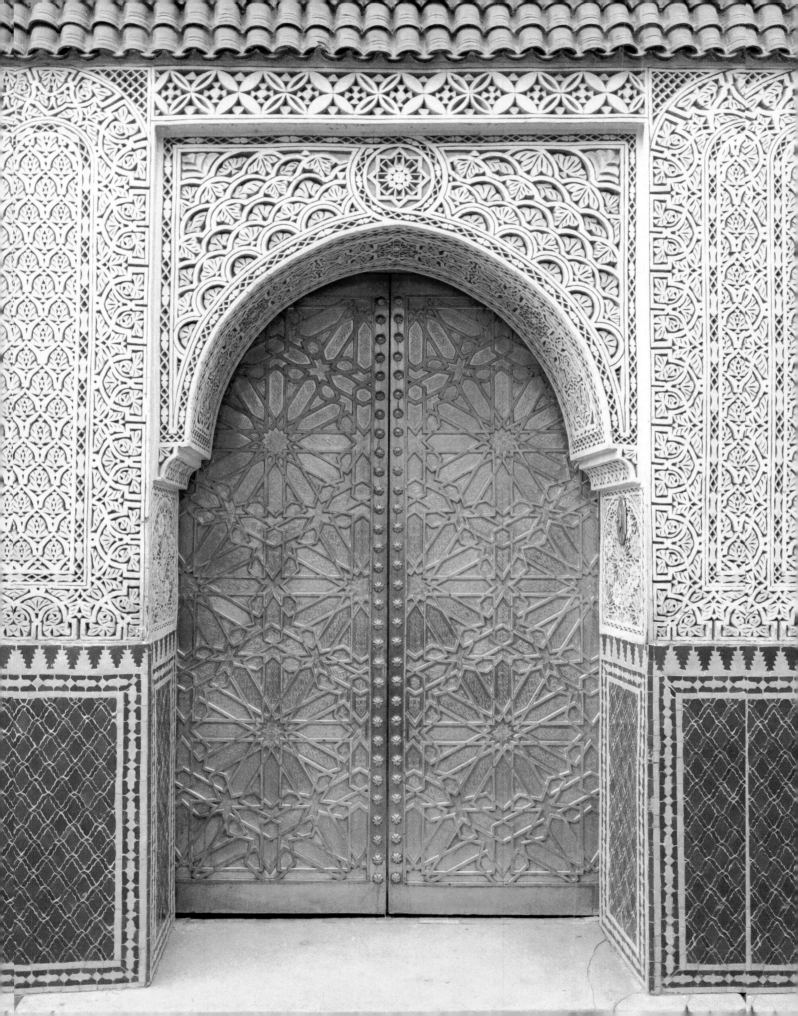

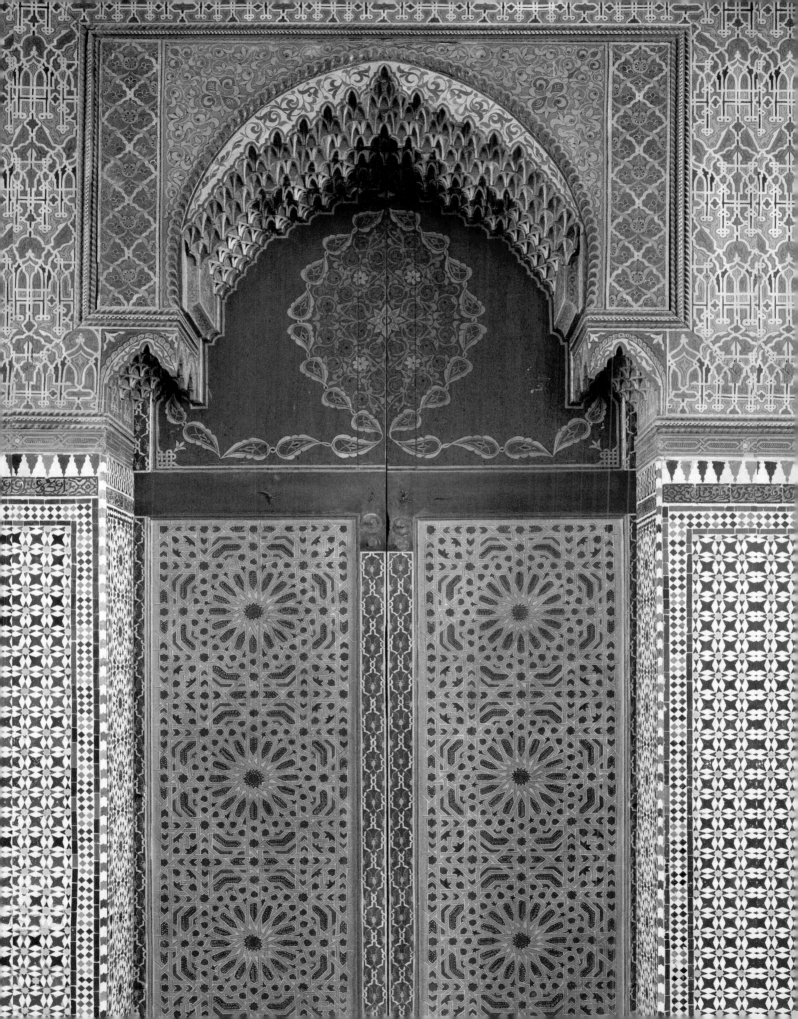

An ABC of Quotes About Palestine: Exploring Voices on Palestine & the Palestinian Quest for Justice (2023)

An Abc of Palestine: A Journey To Discover Palestine & The Palestinian People For Kids & Grown Ups (2023)

Palestine: 200+ Cut-Out & Collage Images for Arts & Crafts Activities (2023)

Palestine: 50+ Colouring Activities to Celebrate Palestine & the Palestinian People (2023)

My Journey Through The Most Beautiful Names of Allah: Arabic Reader & Activity Book for Kids: **(Volume 1, 2 & 3)** (2023)

My First Arabic Alphabet & Colouring Book [Arabic for Little Ones] (2023)

My First Arabic Alphabet: Letter Tracing & Colouring Book [Arabic for Little Ones] (2023)

Essential Arabic Readers: Alphabet Letters with Vowels & Pronunciation Symbols, Mosaic Tree Press (2022)

Similar Sounding Letters in Arabic: Essential Arabic Readers (2023)

Essential Arabic Readers: Arabic Alphabet Writing Practice Handbook, Mosaic Tree Press (2023)

Listen, Read & Write: Arabic Alphabet Letter Groups [Essential Arabic Readers] (2023)

My First Arabic Numbers Reader & Colouring Book, Mosaic Tree Press (2023)

My First Arabic Colours: Reader & Activity Book for Kids, Mosaic Tree Press (2023)

My Arabic Animal Alphabet Reader, Arabic for Little Ones, Mosaic Tree Press (2023)

My First Arabic Alphabet Reader [Arabic for Little Ones] (2023)

My Arabic Learning Journals: My Abc Dictionary (English-Arabic), Mosaic Tree Press (2022)

My Arabic Learning Journals: My Abc Dictionary (Arabic- English), Mosaic Tree Press (2022)

My Arabic Learning Journals: Thematic Vocabulary, Mosaic Tree Press (2022)

I Am .... An ABC of Empowering Self-Affirmations: A Guided Journal for Self-Discovery, Self-Growth & Resilience (2022)

My Journey through Ramadan & Eid Al-Fitr (Arabic for Little Ones), Mosaic Tree Press (2023)

CoronaVirus Lexicon: A Practical Guide for Arabic Learners & Translators (M. Diouri & M. Aboelezz 2023)

Arabic & Islamic Mosaic & Calligraphy Colouring Journal (Volume 1: Islamic Quotes) (2022)

Browse our full catalogue at
MosaicTree.org

 Arabic Script & Sounds

 Arabic Vocabulary

 Arabic for Little Ones

 Arabic/Islamic Mosaic & Calligraphy

 Arabic Learning Journals

 Well-Being & Character Development

🌳 **Mosaic Tree Press**
MosaicTree.org

Completed with the grace of God

Printed in Great Britain
by Amazon

43385737R00086